Explore

Colonial Jamestown

with Elaine Landau

Enslow Elementary

an imprint of

Enslow Publishers, Inc.

E

40 Industrial Road   PO Box 38
Box 398   Aldershot
Berkeley Heights, NJ 07922   Hants GU12 6BP
USA   UK

http://www.enslow.com

For the Gjertsen Gang.

Enslow Elementary, an imprint of Enslow Publishers, Inc.

Enslow Elementary® is a registered trademark of Enslow Publishers, Inc.

Library of Congress Cataloging-in-Publication Data:

Landau, Elaine.
    Explore Colonial Jamestown with Elaine Landau / Elaine Landau.
        p. cm. — (Explore Colonial America with Elaine Landau)
    Includes bibliographical references and index.
    ISBN-10: 0-7660-2554-3
    1. Jamestown (Va.)—History—17th century—Juvenile literature. 2. Jamestown (Va.)—Biography—Juvenile literature. 3. Virginia—History—Colonial period, ca. 1600–1775—Juvenile literature. I. Title.
II. Series.
F234.J3L36 2006
973.2'1—dc22   2005008382

ISBN-13: 978-0-7660-2554-7

Printed in the United States of America

10 9 8 7 6 5 4 3 2

To Our Readers: We have done our best to make sure all Internet Addresses in this book were active and appropriate when we went to press. However, the author and the publisher have no control over and assume no liability for the material available on those Internet sites or on other Web sites they may link to. Any comments or suggestions can be sent by e-mail to comments@enslow.com or to the address on the back cover.

Series Literacy Consultant: Allan A. De Fina, Ph.D., Past President of the New Jersey Reading Association and Professor, Department of Literacy Education, New Jersey City University.

Illustration Credits: © Corel Corporation, p. 17; Courtesy of APVA Preservation Virginia, p. 38; Dave Pavelonis, Elaine and Max illustrations on pp. 1, 3, 5, 6, 7, 9, 12, 14, 19, 23, 25, 27, 31, 35, 39, 41, 42; Elaine Landau, p. 42; Enslow Publishers, Inc., pp. 4–5 (map), 8, 20; Getty Images, pp. 6, 13, 15, 16 (top), 18, 28, 32, 33, 34; Hemera Technologies, Inc./Enslow Publishers, Inc./Library of Congress, backgrounds on pp. 3–7, 42–48; © Jeffrey Greenberg/The Image Works, p. 11; © Joe Sohm/The Image Works, pp. 24 (bottom), 25; J.S. Peterson @ USDA-NRCS PLANTS Database, p. 30; Judith Edwards, pp. 1, 12, 16 (bottom), 27, 39, 40, 44 (bottom); The Library of Congress, pp. 21, 31, 43 (top); National Geographic Society/Getty Images, p. 36; NOAA, p. 5 (Chesapeake coastline); Painet Works, pp. 2, 7, 10, 26; Photodisc, p. 4 (ships); Photos.com, pp. 9, 19; © Public Record Office/Topham-HIP/The Image Works, p. 23; Reproduced from the *Dictionary of American Portraits*, published by Dover Publications, Inc., in 1967, pp. 22, 29, 43 (bottom), 44 (top); U.S. Fish and Wildlife Service, p. 24 (top).

Front Cover Illustrations: Dave Pavelonis (Elaine & Max); Getty Images (Settlers landing).

Back Cover Illustrations: Dave Pavelonis (Elaine & Max); Painet Works (ship).

Contents

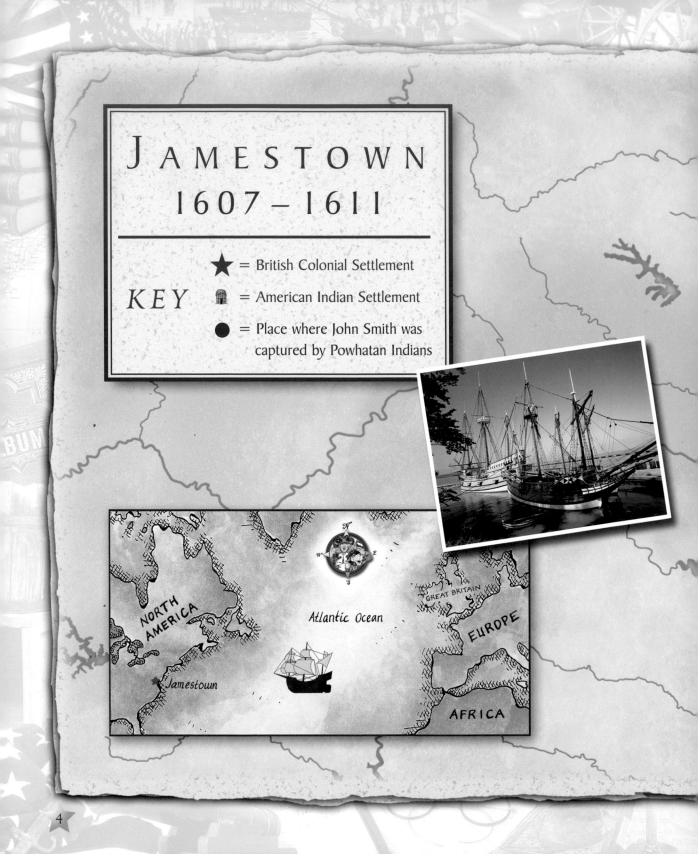

JAMESTOWN
1607 – 1611

KEY

★ = British Colonial Settlement

▯ = American Indian Settlement

● = Place where John Smith was captured by Powhatan Indians

NORTH AMERICA

Atlantic Ocean

GREAT BRITAIN

EUROPE

Jamestown

AFRICA

Potomac River

Rappahannock River

Mattaponi River

Pamunkey River

James River

Chickahominy River

Smith Captured

Henrico

York River

Appomattox River

Jamestown

James River

Chesapeake Bay

Cape Charles

Smith's Island

Point Comfort

Cape Henry

Atlantic Ocean

Dear Fellow Explorer,

What if you could travel back in time? Would you want to visit an early American colony? You could see what life was like in a new land.

Imagine being a settler in Jamestown, Virginia. That was the first permanent English colony in North America. Would you want to stay and help build

This map shows the Jamestown settlement in 1608. The buildings were inside a fort. The long wooden wall around the fort is called a palisade.

The settlers used a cannon to defend themselves from their enemies. Actors playing settlers stand near an entrance to a recreated fort at Jamestown Settlement.

the colony? Or would you play it safe and catch the next ship back to Britain?

I am Elaine Landau and this is my dog Max. Max and I are taking a trip back in time to Jamestown. Come along with us. There is a lot to see. Are you ready to start your **journey**? Just turn the page . . .

1 An Exciting Plan

In the early 1600s, few Europeans had been to North America. However, they had heard exciting tales about this wild new world. Explorers described it as a rich paradise.

Some English settlers had gone to North America in the late 1500s. Twice they tried to start a settlement on Roanoke Island. This is an island in the area we know today as North Carolina. (Back then, it was part of Virginia.) Both attempts failed. So, in 1600 there were still no English settlements in North America.

People in England knew of the failed settlements. Yet, some still longed to cross the Atlantic. They wanted to go for different reasons.

Religion was an important reason to go. The Church of England wanted to bring the Christian religion to the American Indians.

Great Britain's King James I also wanted glory. Britain's rivals—France and Spain—had

King James I encouraged his people to settle North America.

settlements in North America. Britain's king wanted his share of this land.

The hope of discovering great riches drew many others to the New World. Some dreamed of finding gold and jewels.

Spices were worth much more money in 1607 than they are today. This is because spices came from Asia and Indonesia. This was a part of the world that was once very hard for people to get to.

Still others sought a quicker route to Asia for jewels, silks, and spices. Spices add flavor to food. They also help to keep meat fresh. Was there a shorter way to reach Asia from Britain? Some hoped to find a sea route through North America.

The Virginia Company of London dreamed of building a thriving colony in North America. There was money to be made across the sea. The company had received permission from King James I to start a settlement. By December 1606, the company was set to do exactly that. They had found a group of people that were ready to brave the Atlantic Ocean and three sturdy ships to take them to what was then called the New World.

DO YOU THINK THE VIRGINIA COMPANY WILL MAKE A LOT OF MONEY?

BUILDING A COLONY IS HARD WORK. EVEN THE SUCCESSFUL ONES DIDN'T MAKE A PROFIT RIGHT AWAY.

② Setting Out

From England (part of Britain), 144 people would make the first trip for the Virginia Company. Of the group, 104 were settlers and the rest were crew— all men.

The group left on December 20, 1606, in three ships. These were the *Discovery*, the *Godspeed*, and the *Susan Constant*. Captain Christopher Newport was in charge of the voyage.

The difficult trip across the Atlantic took about four months. There were storms at sea. Much of the food rotted. Some of the passengers became ill. Also, the ships made stops at a few islands in the Caribbean Sea. This was far south from where they were

This ship at Jamestown Settlement museum was built to look like the original *Susan Constant*.

These actors are playing sailors on a recreated *Susan Constant* at Jamestown Settlement. Sailors often stayed in Jamestown while their ships were there.

supposed to land in Virginia. They were glad to finally reach land in the early morning of April 26, 1607. Yet it took another two weeks to pick a site for the colony.

On May 14, they settled on a place they named Jamestown Island. It was on the James River, about sixty miles from the mouth of Chesapeake Bay. This was in the region we now call Virginia. Jamestown Island was not really an island but was actually a **peninsula** (pen•in•sue•la). That is a section of land surrounded by water on three sides. Only a very thin strip of land connected it to the rest of Virginia.

Captain Newport and the others liked the spot. The water around the peninsula was deep. Their ships could be brought near the shore. That made loading and unloading vessels easier.

The new land also offered some protection from Indian attacks. It was almost completely surrounded by water. That made it much easier to defend.

The colony would be safe from Britain's enemies as well. Jamestown was near the Atlantic Ocean. Lookouts could be posted to spot

The Powhatan Indians used poles like this in their ceremonies. Sometimes they had a ceremony before they went to war.

When the first settlers landed at Jamestown, they did not know what to expect.

approaching ships from Spain or other countries unfriendly toward Britain.

The settlers thought they had made a good choice. Unfortunately, they would soon find out that they had not. There were some things they had not considered. Hard times were ahead for this adventurous group of English colonists.

③ A Poor Choice

Jamestown was not what the settlers had in mind. The peninsula had many marshy areas. These were filled with stale dirty water. As a result, there were a lot of mosquitoes. The mosquitoes carried disease. Frequent flooding on the peninsula made things worse.

The settlers had no clean drinking water. The James River's water was **brackish** (salty). It was not fit to drink. The more the settlers drank it, the more thirsty they became. It even made the people sick.

There were other problems too. More than half the settlers were British "gentlemen" who were not used to hard work. They were only interested in getting rich by finding gold or by trading things they found to Britain. The other settlers were mostly skilled craftsmen. They could make tools, weapons, jewelry, and other useful items. Only a few men had farming skills.

There was also no strong leader at Jamestown. The Virginia

LET'S GET OUT OF THIS MARSH AND AWAY FROM THESE MOSQUITOES.

YEAH, I'M BEING EATEN ALIVE!

Jamestown settlers were always in danger of an American Indian attack. The Indians were defending their land against the settlers.

Company had picked a group of men to form a government. Among those chosen to serve on the **governing council** was John Smith. During the voyage, he had been disrespectful to the English gentlemen. Captain Newport even charged him with rebellion and some wanted to hang him. Now he was to be one of their leaders. One of the reasons he was picked was that he had experience as a leader. Before the voyage, Smith had led other soldiers as a captain in the army.

Life at Jamestown was not easy. Right away, more than two hundred Paspahegh Indians attacked the settlement. The settlers were unprepared. They had not even finished building their fort.

John Smith had fought in many battles before he settled in Jamestown.

The settlers quickly ran to one of their ships for

This yahakin in Jamestown Settlement's recreated Powhatan village was the type of house used by the Powhatan Indians.

The American Indians had their own ways of survival. The main vegetable they ate was corn. This modern woman prepares food the way the American Indians did.

protection. They fired their muskets and cannons from there. These were weapons that the American Indians did not have. Even if the settlers did not hit their attackers, the sound of the guns often scared the Indians away at first. Nevertheless, one settler was killed. Eleven others were wounded.

This marked the start of a troubled time between the settlers and the different groups of American Indians that lived in the area. Sometimes there would be peace and friendship. Other years were filled with war and much bloodshed.

4 A Dream Gone Wrong

The settlers hoped for the best. Yet the summer of 1607 was terrible. A large number of the settlers became deathly ill.

Some settlers had malaria, a serious disease spread by mosquitoes. Others suffered from typhoid. This is an illness caused by germs in food and water. Many settlers got sick drinking impure river water.

Not many crops had been planted and the supply ships from England were late. The settlers were weak and hungry.

A fort was built around the settlement to protect the settlers from attack.

During the summer, death became common at Jamestown. Often, several

settlers died on the same day. At times, those who lived barely had the strength to bury the dead.

The fall brought cooler weather. Yet by then, more than half of the original settlers were dead.

Jamestown badly needed good leaders. But most on the governing council were not up to the task. The real hero at Jamestown proved to be John Smith.

Smith began trading with the Paspaheghs. The Paspaheghs gave the settlers bread and corn. In return, the settlers gave the Paspaheghs **trinkets** and other items.

With food in their stomachs, the settlers felt better. However, there were fewer of them now. Even the English gentlemen had to work.

Smith made everyone farm. They also had to finish the buildings they had started. Life was better at Jamestown, but not for long.

THAT JOHN SMITH IS A GOOD TRADER.

YES. HE WAS ABLE TO GET MUCH NEEDED FOOD AFTER MANY OF THE SETTLERS HAD DIED.

The American Indians had enough corn to trade with the Jamestown settlers. Corn could be dried and ground into a powder called corn meal. The corn meal could then be used to make bread.

5 Smith and Powhatan

There was a powerful Indian leader in the Jamestown area named Powhatan. More than thirty groups or tribes answered to him. Powhatan's group were named the Powhatan Indians, after him. Powhatan did not like the settlers. He saw them as **invaders**.

In December 1607, John Smith left Jamestown with a small group of men. He wanted to explore the surrounding **region**, or area. While away, the group was attacked by Powhatan Indians. Some of Smith's men were killed but Smith was taken captive.

Smith was brought before the great chief Powhatan. He enjoyed a feast with the American Indians. Then two stones were brought out. They were placed in front of Powhatan.

At that point, things did not look good for Smith. He was dragged over to the stones and thrown on the ground. The Indians placed Smith's head on the stones. They stood above Smith with raised clubs.

Powhatan was a leader of a large group of American Indians.

John Smith was sure that he was going to die. He thought that the Indians were about to crush his skull.

Just at that moment, an Indian girl named Pocahontas came running out. She was only about twelve years old. Pocahontas was Powhatan's favorite daughter. She begged her father to stop his men. But the chief would not listen.

So Pocahontas raced over to Smith and put her head on his. If John Smith died, she would too. Powhatan told his men to put their clubs down. Pocahontas had saved John Smith's life.

The story John Smith told of his first meeting with Powhatan is famous. However, we do not know if it is true. Many historians think that Pocahontas actually may not have saved John Smith's life.

Smith often told stories that made him look brave or important.

Pocahontas probably did meet John Smith that evening. But what she really did that night is not clear. Some people think that Pocahontas did not act on her own. They believe that her father told her to save Smith.

Powhatan was a very wise chief. He may have known that killing a Jamestown leader was a bad idea. Perhaps he wanted John Smith to owe him a favor.

This portrait of Pocahontas shows her in European clothes.

Smith returned to Jamestown. A few days later, Pocohantas brought food to the colony. By then, the harsh winter of 1608 had set in. The settlers were grateful for her help.

They were less pleased with John Smith. Many of the gentlemen were angry at having to work. Others blamed Smith for the deaths of the men he went exploring with. The governing council sentenced John Smith to hang.

Yet, John Smith's life was spared again. This time Captain Newport rescued him. On January 4, 1608, Newport returned to the colony from England. He brought supplies and more settlers. Newport had Smith released. He knew that Smith got along well with the

American Indians. The captain felt that the colony needed Smith alive.

It was a good decision. On January 7, 1608, a terrible fire swept through Jamestown. It destroyed the settlers' homes, food, and supplies. After the fire, the Indians brought them more food.

> **LOOKS LIKE CAPTAIN NEWPORT SAVED THE DAY.**

> **YES! YEARS LATER, THE SETTLEMENT OF NEWPORT NEWS WAS NAMED AFTER HIM.**

By spring, the colony had been rebuilt. Captain Newport again left for England. The settlers planted new crops and hoped for much better times.

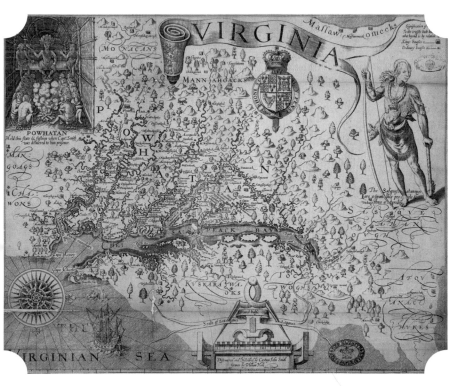

John Smith explored much of the area surrounding Jamestown. He later published his own map of Virginia.

6 Changes at Jamestown

In September 1608, John Smith became president of the governing council. He divided the men into work crews. The crews fished, farmed, and chopped down trees for lumber. Some lumber was used for buildings in the colony. Lumber was also sent back to England to be sold there.

In October, Captain Newport brought more settlers. Among them were the colony's first women. John Smith put them to work, too. Smith also made the men train with weapons. Dealings with the Indians had become less friendly. Smith expected more trouble.

The settlers often ate a certain type of fish called Atlantic sturgeon. Remains of sturgeon have been found at the Jamestown site.

A Jamestown settler had to do hard work. This man, who is pretending to be a settler, gathers straw for the roofs of houses.

The settlement did well under Smith's leadership. Yet, the colony still had not begun to earn a **profit**. So the Virginia Company made some changes. It did away with the governing council. Instead, a governor would be put in charge.

John Smith also had a bad accident. A sack of gunpowder exploded, badly injuring him. He returned to England in the summer of 1609. The settlement would not be the same without John Smith.

The houses at Jamestown were small but kept the colonists safe from bad weather. The houses pictured are at the Jamestown Settlement museum.

7 The Starving Time

After John Smith left, there was no real leadership at Jamestown. The new governor still had not arrived. People did not work as hard as they should have.

Things grew worse between the settlers and the American Indians. Powhatan no longer traded with the settlers. Now fear replaced friendship. Any settler who left the fort was attacked. The men were afraid to fish or hunt. They felt like prisoners in their own colony.

This led to the worst months in Jamestown's history. The winter of 1609–1610 was known as "the starving time." Settlers had almost nothing to eat. They killed and ate their horses. They even ate the rats they caught.

People died of starvation and disease daily. Some used their last bit of strength to dig their own graves. There had been about five

During the "starving time," there was not much for the Jamestown settlers to cook. Here, an actor playing a colonist washes laundry at Jamestown Settlement museum.

hundred Jamestown settlers before that winter. Only about sixty were left by the spring of 1610.

THE STARVING TIME WAS TERRIBLE. I JUST HOPE NO ONE ATE ANY DOGS.

LET'S NOT EVEN THINK ABOUT THAT, MAX.

Several ships carrying new settlers arrived in May 1610. The newcomers were shocked at what they found. The survivors looked like walking skeletons. Little was left of the colony as well. The remaining settlers had taken apart most of the buildings.

An actor pretending to be a settler tends to an old-fashioned stone oven as part of a glass-blowing demonstration at Historic Jamestowne.

They used the lumber for firewood. It was all they had to keep warm during the winter.

The survivors were anxious to leave Jamestown. The new arrivals wanted to leave too. They saw that there was no food.

After the "starving time," ships with food, supplies, and more colonists arrived at Jamestown.

Yet as it turned out, none of them left. The very next morning,

another ship arrived with food and supplies. A man named Lord De La Warr was on it. He was the colony's new governor.

Like John Smith, De La Warr quickly took charge. People planted crops and rebuilt houses. Nevertheless, De La Warr left the colony in March 1611 because of poor health. He had not lasted a year at Jamestown.

The next leader arrived in Jamestown on May 19, 1611. He was a former soldier named Sir Thomas Dale. The Virginia Company wanted Dale to find a better site for the settlement. Dale chose a spot upriver that was not as marshy as Jamestown. Today it is known as Curles Neck. Back then, it was called Henrico.

In the short time that he was governor, Lord De La Warr helped the colonists get organized.

American Indians were already living in that area. That did not matter to Dale. He fought the Indians and took their land. Dale saw this as Britain's right. The Indians saw things differently. This would lead to problems later.

8 Jamestown Still Remained

The Henrico settlement grew. Other Virginia settlements were started as well. However, Jamestown was not deserted. Settlers remained there. One named John Rolfe began planting tobacco at Jamestown.

In time, more settlers came to Virginia. Before long, they outnumbered the American Indians there. At times the settlers killed the Indians to get their land and corn.

British settlers also kidnapped Pocahontas in 1613. She was about sixteen years old at the time.

The settlers had been anxious to get Powhatan's daughter. They expected him to give them corn and other things to get her back. At first, Powhatan agreed to the settlers' demands. However, the colonists never received what they wanted. Meanwhile, Pocahontas became a Christian. On April 5, 1614, she also married one of the settlers—the tobacco grower John Rolfe.

Tobacco is still grown in Virginia today.

Both settlers and Powhatan Indians went to the wedding of Pocahontas and John Rolfe.

As time passed, Jamestown had different leaders. The Virginia Company picked the governors. But all this changed in July 1619. At point, the colonists got to pick their own leaders. This new group of leaders was known as the House of Burgesses. Twenty-two men were **elected** to represent the settlers.

The House of Burgesses was the first elected government in North America. It passed many different laws. Some laws were about proper behavior. Others had to do with the American Indians. Still

JAMESTOWN HAS AN ELECTED GOVERNMENT. WHAT A HISTORIC DAY!

THE UNITED STATES STILL HAS AN ELECTED GOVERNMENT TODAY. IT'S CALLED CONGRESS.

other laws involved deciding how much people should pay for tobacco.

Between 1619 and 1622, Jamestown grew. More women arrived. Soon, there were families at Jamestown.

Many people began growing tobacco. More land was needed for this. So the settlers spread out. They started large tobacco growing farms called **plantations**.

Numerous tobacco growers did quite well. Yet their lives were not problem-free. Before long there was more trouble with the American Indians.

Powhatan had died in 1618. Another strong leader had taken over. His name was Opechancanough (o-pech-un-kano). Opechancanough did not like the

Men load barrels of tobacco onto a ship. Ships brought tobacco to Britain where it was sold or traded.

Settlers had to make their own bricks for building houses. The bricks were made of mud, straw, and other things and laid out in the sun to dry.

English either. They had taken too much land and treated his people badly.

On March 22, 1622, Opechancanough struck back. He and his men staged an early morning attack. The settlers were caught off guard. Some were killed at the breakfast table. Others were struck down while working in the fields. Opechancanough's men killed 347 settlers. That was about one third of the colony. The Indians also burned the settlers' homes, plantations, and ironworks.

By now, the Virginia Company had grown weary. Jamestown was always plagued by problems. King James I was disappointed, too. He took away the company's charter, which was the agreement the colony had with the Virginia Company. Jamestown simply became a British colony. The Virginia Company no longer had a claim to it.

9 Closing Time

Time passed, and life at Jamestown became fairly normal. By the 1640s, many craftsmen and merchants had shops there. The colony had glassblowers, carpenters, jewelry makers, weavers, and winemakers. Some of the richer families had large two-story brick homes.

There were also more tobacco plantations nearby. Settlers no longer feared starving. Enough food was grown each year. The bad times seemed to be over.

The colonists had to grow or make most of everything they needed. Here, a Jamestown settler makes pots out of clay.

However, in April 1644, Opechancanough struck again. It was another surprise attack. This time about five hundred settlers were killed. Some escaped to nearby forts that had been built. Many refused to return to their homes for months. They were afraid of another attack.

The trouble between the American Indians and the settlers continued. At times, the settlers disagreed on how to deal with the native people. This led to fighting among themselves.

All the fighting weakened Jamestown. Many people moved to a nearby settlement, Middle Plantation. The area would later be called Williamsburg.

By the late 1690s, few people lived in Jamestown anymore. It was no longer a center for trade or business.

In 1698, much of what was left of the settlement was destroyed in a fire. Yet that small struggling colony has not been forgotten. Jamestown has a special place in our nation's history.

10 Heading Home

Today, much of Jamestown has been rebuilt on a different site from where it originally was. The new site, called Jamestown Settlement, looks much like the colony did four hundred years ago. Visitors can see the fort, houses, craft shops, and even a rebuilt American Indian village. Tour guides there dress as the early settlers did. They tell about the colony's history.

Archeologists at the original Jamestown site, now called Historic Jamestowne, have uncovered items colonists used. Archeologists are people who dig up old

Archeologists at Historic Jamestowne work on uncovering the bottom part of the Jamestown colony's fort.

Some Early Jamestown Settlers

The information on this list came from the writings of John Smith and other records of the history of early Virginia.

NAME	DESCRIPTION	DATE OF ARRIVAL
Captain John Ratcliffe	**Captain of the** *Discovery* **and President of the Governing Council**—The council was made up of the colony's leaders.	May 13, 1607
Master Robert Hunt	**Preacher**—The preacher ran the church services in Jamestown. The settlers were members of the Church of England, a Christian church. By May 1610, they had lost their preacher, since Robert Hunt had died by then.	May 13, 1607
Thomas Wotton	**Gentleman** and **Surgeon**—The "gentlemen" who came to Jamestown were rich men. They often wanted to become richer. Many of them did not want to do any work. Thomas Wotton was different because he was a special type of doctor called a surgeon.	May 13, 1607
Robert Small	**Carpenter**—Carpenters built homes and the colony's fort.	May 13, 1607
James Read	**Blacksmith**—Blacksmiths made useful tools and weapons out of metal. Read was later hanged for threatening the life of John Ratcliffe.	May 13, 1607
William Love	**Tailor**—The colony tailor made and repaired clothes.	May 13, 1607
John Dods	**Laborer**—Laborers cut down trees to make homes. They also did many other things that required hard work.	May 13, 1607
William Dawson	**Refiner**—Refiners removed metals from rock. The blacksmith melted these metals and made them into tools and weapons.	January 1608
Peter Keffer	**Gunner**—The settlers had to protect themselves from attackers. Many of the men in the colony had already fought in battles. Peter Keffer's job was to guard the colony's fort.	January 1608
Thomas Feld	**Apothecary**—**Apothecaries** provided medicines to help heal people. The apothecaries at Jamestown learned many herbal cures from American Indians.	January 1608
John Lewes	**Cooper**—Coopers made barrels. The barrels were used to ship goods back to Britain for sale or trade.	January 1608
Hugh Wynne	**Tradesman**—Tradesmen traded goods with the American Indians or Britain for things of value that the settlers needed.	Fall 1608
Mrs. Forrest	Mrs. Forrest and her maid, Anne Burras, were the first women to arrive in Jamestown. Mrs. Forrest was married to Thomas Forrest , a gentleman, and died shortly after she arrived. Anne Burras later married John Laydon, a laborer.	Fall 1608

This archeologist is carefully removing a piece of armor from the ground at Historic Jamestowne.

These tools were once used by the Jamestown settlers to build their houses. At the top is part of an ax.

This armor was dug up at Historic Jamestowne. There is a helmet and a breastplate. The armor once protected a settler from American Indian arrows.

objects to study the past. This has helped us know even more about the settlers' exciting lives.

Max and I enjoyed our visit to Jamestown. But we really must be heading home. Max is not used to visiting swampy areas. He wants to soak in a warm tub. I may do the same. We are glad you saw Jamestown with us. There were some tough times, but what an exciting adventure! Time travel is always more fun with friends. Thank you for joining us. To the time machine!

The remains of the Jamestown Church can still be seen today.

Whatever Happened to . . .

Max and I meet a lot of people while time traveling. If you are curious about what became of them, read on.

John Smith

After his injury in 1609, John Smith never returned to Virginia. He made another trip to North America in 1614 to explore New England. Before his death in 1621, John Smith wrote a number of books. Some told of his adventures in Jamestown.

John Smith thought that fish, furs, and lumber were the best products Virginia had to offer.

Pocahontas

Pocahontas and her husband, John Rolfe, and son visited Britain in 1616. While there, Pocahontas met the king and queen. Pocahontas's visit made people more aware of the Jamestown colony. In March 1617, Pocahontas and her family boarded a ship to return to

This statue of Pocahontas stands near the original Jamestown site.

Virginia. However, Pocahontas soon became very ill. She was taken ashore to Gravesend, England. She died there on March 21, 1617.

Opechancanough

Following the 1644 uprising, Opechancanough was captured. He had been caught once before but escaped. This time he was not as lucky. While imprisoned at Jamestown, he was murdered. Some say that a prison guard killed him. After his death, the Powhatan Indians were forced to sign a peace treaty. It gave the settlers even more of the Indians' land.

THE COLLEGE OF WILLIAM AND MARY WAS FOUNDED IN 1693 IN WILLIAMSBURG, VIRGINIA.

THAT'S RIGHT NEAR JAMESTOWN! WHO KNEW THAT AN IMPORTANT COLLEGE WOULD BE BUILT LESS THAN NINETY YEARS AFTER THE FIRST SETTLERS LANDED?!

Farewell Fellow Explorer,

Just wanted to take a moment to tell you a little about the real "Max and me." I am a children's book author and Max is a small, fluffy, white dog. I almost named him Marshmallow because of how he looked. However, he seems to think he's human—so only a more dignified name would do. Max also seems to think that he is a large, powerful dog. He fearlessly chases after much larger dogs in the neighborhood. Max was thrilled when the artist for this book drew him as a dog several times his size. He felt that someone in the art world had finally captured his true spirit.

In real life, Max is quite a traveler. I've taken him to nearly every state while doing research for different books. We live in Florida so when we go north I have to pack a sweater for him. When we were in Oregon it rained and I was glad I brought his raincoat. None of this gear is necessary when time traveling. My "take off" spot is the computer station and as always Max sits faithfully by my side.

Best Wishes,
Elaine & Max
(a small dog with big dreams)

Timeline

Late 1500s—Two Roanoke Island settlements fail.

1606—The Virginia Company of London prepares to start a settlement in the New World.

1607—The settlers arrive at Jamestown Island on May 14.

1608—A terrible fire sweeps through the colony on January 7.

In September, John Smith becomes president of the governing council.

1609—John Smith is wounded that summer when a sack of gunpowder explodes. He goes back to England.

1609–1610—The winter months were known as The Starving Time. Many Jamestown settlers died from lack of food.

1610—Lord De La Warr arrives in Jamestown in May.

1611—Lord De La Warr leaves Jamestown in March.

Sir Thomas Dale arrives in Jamestown in May.

1613—Pocahontas is kidnapped by the English settlers.

Lord De La Warr

Timeline

1614— Pocahontas marries John Rolfe.

1617— Pocahontas dies.

1618— Powhatan dies.

1619— Jamestown's House of Burgesses is started in July.

1622— Opechancanough attacks, killing 347 settlers.

1644— Opechancanough launches a second major attack. This time 500 settlers are killed.

1690— Few people remain in Jamestown.

1698— Jamestown is destroyed in a fire.

1994— Archeological digs begin at Jamestown to recover items from the colony.

Words to Know

apothecary—A person who provides medicines to heal the sick.

archeologist—Someone who learns about the past by digging up and studying old buildings and objects.

captive—A prisoner.

charter—An agreement and/or document.

disasters—Events that cause a lot of loss and suffering.

elected—Chosen to be a leader by the people one will represent.

governing council—A government used by the early Jamestown settlers. The leaders of the governing council were picked by the Virginia Company, not elected by the colonists.

invaders—People who fight to take over another country.

journey—A long trip.

peninsula—An area of land surrounded by water on three sides.

plantation—A large farm.

profit—Money gained.

trinkets—Small items that some people find valuable.

Further Reading

Broida, Marian. *Projects About Colonial Life*. Tarrytown, N.Y.: Benchmark Books, 2004.

DeCapua, Sarah. *The Virginia Colony*. Chanhassen, Minn.: Child's World, 2004.

Doak, Robin S. *Smith: John Smith and the Settlement of Jamestown*. Minneapolis: Compass Point Books, 2003.

Fritz, Jean and Preston, Thomas. *The Lost Colony of Roanoke*. New York: Putnam, 2004.

Isaacs, Sally Senzell. *Life in a Colonial Town*. Chicago: Heinemann, 2000.

January, Brendan. *The Jamestown Colony*. Minneapolis: Compass Point Books, 2001.

Knowlton, Marylee and Riehecky, Janet. *The Settling of Jamestown*. Milwaukee: Garth Stevens, 2002.

Stefoff, Rebecca. *The Colonies*. Tarrytown, N.Y.: Benchmark Books, 2000.

Zemlicka, Shannon. *Pocahontas*. Minneapolis: Carolrhoda, 2002.

Web Sites

Jamestown Rediscovery

<http://www.apva.org>

Visit the site of the archeological project at Jamestown. See pictures of the interesting items found and learn about the latest discoveries.

Virtual Jamestown

<http://www.virtualjamestown.org>

This is a wonderful online history site about the Jamestown settlement. Do not miss the map section for a great view of original maps of Virginia.

Welcome to Jamestown

<http://www.ab.mec.edu/jamestown/jamestown.html>

This site provides a detailed overview of what life was like for early Jamestown settlers. There is lots of information on village life, celebrations, and survival.

Index